My Soul .... . My Life .... . Wouldn't be complete without mentioning My Life.... . This first book of my poems is dedicated to my mom and dad, my partner - Majid, my shining star Aayan, Tabassum, Mohammed & little Zain.
To my family, near and far, and my friends who stand steadfast by my side. To one and all who have played a part in bringing my soul to life.

Tarannum .

My Soul.... .My Life.... .

MY SOUL.... .MY LIFE.... .

My Soul .... . My Life .... . is a collection of reflections and musings on various aspects of life, relationships, emotions, and experiences.

It touches upon feelings related to love, pain, emptiness, trust, relationships, distance, and more. The poems are lyrical and introspective, exploring the depth of emotions and personal reflections. The order of the poems aims to create a cohesive journey through relationships, individual experiences, internal reflections, and a sense of closure

PREFACE

As an individual who always wanted to write a book for a very long time. Each time the thought crossed my mind, I didn't know where to start and what to share. How will it look? How will it compile? How will my thoughts relate?

Every time I pen down my thoughts, every time it flows in words, my soul reminds me of the precious moments in this journey of life. And I feel that one day I will gather all these into a collection to cherish.

Somewhere these poems will touch your soul as you read and it will take you down the memory lane reminding you of the time you spend with your soul mate, with your loved ones, with your life.

I always wanted to gather these emotions together so that someday I have something to look upon. So when my heart touched my soul, I gathered myself to put them together for it to reach from mine to yours.

What better way to express love for someone who is in essence from here to eternity.

My Soul.... .My Life.... .

MY SOUL.... .MY LIFE.... .

MY SOUL.... .MY LIFE.... .

A Reflection Of Our Journey

A journey we began together,
A journey we traversed together.
We held our hands so that the steps don't change,
We walked together so the path remains unchanged.

You were the reflection of my shadow,
You were the echo of my silence;
You were the string that bonded us,
You were the soul of my melting heart.

I held you high,
You were the star of my sky;
Like a lining in the silver moon,
Shinning bright in the dark night.

You were the hope of my thoughts,
You were the tranquil of my mind.
You were the depth of the waters,
You were the denseness of the woods.

When my day dawned with you,
It showered its rays on;
When dusk fell upon,
Your reflection lighted up my heart.

Such was the magic of the day that night kept wandering,
And when it was shimmering in the sky, the sun awaited its rise.

My light you need to stand tall,
Your journey has just begun.
I may be far, but you need to walk,
I may be gone but you need to search;
I may be perished but you need to rise.

For the journey we traversed together,
For the journey we will cherish forever;
For a Life with infinite trust,
For a Soul with divine charm.
For a reflection of thousand mirrors,
For along the journey, we shed infinite tears.

My Soul.... .My Life.... .

The road that we travelled together is our journey of life,
those moments when we held our hands, carefree,
with a feeling of oneness, a feeling of togetherness,
where the world is left behind.

Let the light of our life be burning no matter how dark the road ahead is.

Whichever path you take ahead in life turn back, wait,
let my presence touch your soul, let my warmth be felt,
let my heart be there where your feet felt lonely.

Let us behold our lives together,
let us walk our paths together not with any restrain,
not with any resentment, not with any agony.

Let our path be destined to love, to cherish, to forgive, to understand, to heal.

Let not belief turn to disbelief.
Let not understandings turn to explanations.
Let not acceptance turn into compulsion.
Let not silence turn to words.
Let love be life, let life be love.

Let the footprints on our path be engraved in our hearts,
let it not be vanished in this world and ever after.

Let's not say till death do us part, say even when death do us part.

Let there be tear, but let there be love,
Let you be alone, still let there be me,
Let there be anger, still let there be that smile.
Let there be no life, still let there be soul.

Let our paths lead to our hearts.

My Soul.... .My Life.... .

Paths

Relations

You and Me.

The creator of Life who made us has given ample of things known and unknown.

We meet, we greet, we bosom and know the good and bad of it.

We don't realise the good for you is bad for some,
and the bad in someone is a grace of someone's life.

The Almighty gave us relations with which we are born,
and at the same time he has given us a chance to choose certain.

When you choose Me.
Choose me with my good and bad.
Don't change for me, change with me.
Don't walk along for me , Walk with me.
Don't stand for me stand with me.

Don't love me because you have fallen for it.
Love me because we chose for it.
Don't love me to take it forward all your life,
love me because we are life.
Fight with me not because the world is interfering,
but because we gave a reason to it.

Let it be divine.
So that the divinity of it dazzles our souls.
Let our love be altruistic such that the entire universe glorifies its existence.
Let it be serene such that the world is coerced to apotheosize its candour.
Let's not be jarring only because we are not together in this world.
Let go of haughty attitude, let go of exasperation, let go of jibe someone passes on you.
Not because you are weak, not because you can't rise to the bait.
But because it's not you and me.
It's we, and our purity doesn't require explication.

A reverent silence speaks a thousand words.

Let there be love, just love.
Let there be you, let there be me. Let there be we.

Love is unconditional, love is selfless, love is kind,
it knows no dissidence, it knows no prejudice.

You came, you loved.
We were in sync with our thoughts, our words, our behaviour, our actions.

Moments spend together. Priceless, pure, magical. Close to our souls.

Let not the resentment within for the world spoil the charm of our divinity.

Let love be pure and pious like a child in the womb.

Let it not vent anger for situations which are testing's of life.

Behold before we fall apart. Before the tears dry.
Before the heart cries. Before the soul dies.

Let there be dots not to end but to connect,
to not refrain from completing, fulfilling the silence within, with the language of love.

Love for our souls. Live for ourselves.
Love me as your first love, cherish us till the last breath.

Let love be bliss, let love be eternal, axe out the I within, let there be WE, till eternity.

Let it be love, let it be life.

My Soul.... .My Life.... .

Love

Romance

A day spent with you is a year we lived,
A moment so precious preserved within.
The words we share is the heart that spoke.
Caresses whispered, love felt, words unspoken, tears filled.
Miles to walk, days to pass.

Even though I may not be there besides you,
my breath will cherish your soul.
My fragrance will brighten your day.
My touch will lighten your night.

Maybe life will not have me always around,
Maybe moments will be spent without my words.
Maybe your heart will hear the beat in the bemused ocean of love.
Maybe you will not have footsteps to follow.

I will still be there, just be there.

In the whispering saga of a love which will always be cherished.
In the beat of your heart which will always have my soul alive.
In the freshness of flowers which will remind you of my fragrance.
On the path which you take where my shadow will be your guide.
In the divinity of God where love will always prevail.
In the finiteness of the infinite universe.

I'll be there. In your thoughts, In your soul,
In your actions, In your speech, In your life, As your life.

My Soul.... .My Life.... .

As We echoes within, I feel the togetherness,
As We touches my soul, I feel togetherness,
As We makes Us, I feel togetherness.

Days spend together or alone We are still there,
Moments so magical, memories cherished, we smiled together.
Love We loved you; Life We gave you.
Night as it shimmers, reminiscence of the magic twinkles in my eyes.

Distance is there, path is not lost.
Hearts as they beat, entangled in our soul.
A Bond so strong, a chord so special.
A night so long, in heavens We meet.

Togetherness:
Lies in no bondage, Lies in no fear,
Lies in no difference, Lies in no fracas.

It is:
In our love, in our acceptance;
In our faith, in our wait.

Maybe We are not together,
But We are not apart.
Maybe touch cannot be felt,
But maybe it can be sensed.
Maybe words can't be heard,
But silence is felt.
Maybe eyes long to see,
But fragrance flows within.

Together apart,
As We depart.
Life stays alive, calm beneath.
As Aroma of the Soul flows,
Life stays alive, loud above.

My Soul.... .My Life.... .

Togetherness

Soul

Where our eyes meet out words
Where our pain is felt by heart
Where desires are repressed by silence
Where pleasures are felt in smiles
Where discomfort is seen in exasperation.

Our souls do meet where life begins its new journey.
A destiny to reach the horizon.
Where the sun will rise above it
Where the range of vision magnifies.

I want my calmness to be felt in your actions.
I want my poise to be graced by your expressions.
I want my tears to fill the void.
I want your strength to bridge their world.

Such be the vigour of our love.
That the aura be graced by its scent.
That its presence is ardent to heavens.

Souls be touched by our souls.
Life be felt by life's.

Such is the potential of our hearts.
Such is the mastery of our love.
Such is the bond of our souls.
Such is the truth that prevails.
Such is the tears that roll.

Souls of all souls. Life of all life's.
Seen and unseen. Moving and unmoving.

My Soul.... .My Life.... .

When I hear an echo,
I smile with your thoughts,
When I ponder upon memories,
I gleam of triumph.
When I walk past time,
it tranquilises me in moments,
When I reflect myself,
it mirrors my chimera.

You are the fracas of my words,
You are the bond of my virtue,
You are the brawn for my path,
You are the resolve for my mind.

Such is the aura in the absence,
Such is the strain in the disconnect,
Such is the wrath of the distance,
Such is the havoc of relinquish.

Feel my presence in your power,
Nudge your purpose with my prayers,
Manoeuvre your pave with our poise,
Reach the grail with our candour.

Let not fiasco dampen your ardour,
Let the Essence of Soul be fondled,
Let Life not loose, Let love not wane,
Let We exist, in absence, in abundance.

My Soul.... .My Life.... .

Essence

The Little Me

The curious inquisitive little girl,
The silent sheepish warrior within.
The immature vigorous teen,
The optimistic gleeful countenance.
The tricenarian shining star,
The fervid slant intellect.

The ardent half,
The rejig friend,
The indulgent originator,
The supportive confidant,
The guiding light,
The shielding sight.

The yearning wait,
The devotion illustrious.

That is a journey,
That is the allure,
That is the finesse,
That is a Women.
That is the Substance.

My Soul.... .My Life.... .

A name with various names,
A Mother, Ma, Mumma, Ammi.
A name to be remembered in every form,
A name to cherish at every age.

In my woe you are remembered,
In my glee you are remembered.
In my zest you are there,
In my blues you are there.

Mother a Life, A world for us.
Blessings straight from the sky,
A creation of Almighty,
Teaches Love as She fades by.

A child She bears, A human She makes,
A miracle God bestowed,
A heaven God created on earth.
Home where a mother is,
Heart where a mother stays.
Such is her divinity;
such is her charisma.
A Life She is,
A Life She bears.

A Daughter, A Love, A Wife, A Mother, A Life.
For She has an Era to Live,
Relations to nurture.

From a mother to a mother,
Far though always near,
A journey your reflection.
A Life She lived, A Life She made.

My Soul.... .My Life.... .

Mother

Father

To a man who builds relations,
To a man who nurtures love.
To a man who whispers prayers,
To a man who is the pride.

A relation which is just not by law,
A relation which is just not for name.
A relation which is eternal.

A name doesn't require boundaries,
A bond so eternal.
A knot that won't go loose,
A warmth through thick and thin.
A kiss near or far.

A relation divine,
A man who is always a pride.
A Father who a daughter's first love,
A Father who is a son's first hero.

My Soul.... .My Life.... .

To A Child In Me.
To A Child With Me.
You were born to live;
you were born to love.
The day the world embraced you,
my arms let you free.

To fly in the mighty sky.
To make place for your own congruence.

Let your pride be held high,
But let your feet be crafty.
Let your fame be loud,
But let your speech be suave.
Let your actions be felt,
But let the hearts don't hurt.

Be the child in the man.
Be the pride of the womb.
Let the Creator feel divine in what he formed.
Let His divinity prevail, let Him feel conquered.
Let souls be together, even when we depart.
Let our story be unabridged.

Let divinity be infinite. Let infinity be life.

My Soul.... .My Life.... .

Child

Attachment

A thread which is linked to the womb.
Attachment in detachment

A heart that beats even in pain.
Eyes that are moist even in happiness.
Soul that remains even when gone.
Body which exists even though perished.
A smile that is to stay even when sadness empowers it.

Days to live even when life's apart.
Happiness to give even with a heavy heart.
Love to shower even though its lost.

Rise and shine so that the soul is proud of.
Do not agonise on the world even when you are marred.

Let me be attached to myself even when detached.
Let me be proud to achieve what myself preaches.
Let us celebrate this day as we never did, and we never will.
Let us celebrate the birth of the child from the womb
to be detached from its attachment, yet to live till life persists.

My Soul.... .My Life.... .

To the son who is my heart,
To the boy who is my soul,
To the man who breathes together,
To the love who is nearer than farther.

You were within me a prayer,
You smiled in my world a blessing,
You came into life a gift so pure,
A blessing so divine.

As the year passes by, wishes would unfold,
Yesterday is a memory,
Today is a hope,
Tomorrow is a dream.

Prayers flow from within,
May you be the light of my life,
May you be the breath I endure,
May you be the pride I apprise,
May you be reverential in your actions,
May you still be stark as the sunshine.
Wishes said, prayers flow.

You are the sunshine that makes my day,
You are the twilight that has a saga to say,
You are the hope of my dreams,
You are the strength of my thoughts.

I am there today, I may not be there forever;
But my love we are always together.
As you rise each day you will feel my breath besides,
As you hold you will feel my touch bequeath,
As you shine you will see my tears twinkle.

So, rise as the sun rises to the darkness,
Smile as the stars twinkles with the moon,
Shine; do not halter,
You are indeed a Gift so special,
You are my Pride; you are my Life.

To a son who is my heart, entangled forever.

My Soul.... .My Life.... .

Wishes, Far and Near

Success

A mantra, one's thoughts.

What you feel is success,
maybe a failure for some.
What you feel as winning,
maybc a fate destined.
What you feel is achieving,
maybe a path crafted to follow.
What you feel is the challenge,
maybe it's a test to be taken.

What you feel is right,
maybe it wants you to try.
What you feel is not working,
Maybe
it prevents you from a fall.
What you wished for didn't happen,
maybe you were worthier.

What you feel is darkness,
maybe it's a feeble gleam.
What you feel is the end,
maybe it's the horizon.
What you seek for,
maybe it was not meant to be.
What you wish to achieve,
maybe it would overthrow you.

What you aspire,
maybe its deficient.
What you possess,
maybe its wealthier.
What you feel is failure,
maybe it's the success.

Trust the process, behold the faith.

My Soul.... .My Life.... .

When you trust someone,
it comes from your soul.
There are no limitations of thoughts, words, feelings.

When you speak it's your heart that echoes.
When you behave it's your love that showers.
When you act it's the child in you that impersonates.
When one sets frontiers,
it leads to frailty and qualm in the bond that is divine.

Set yourself unimpeded of vexation, resentment, resistance.

Love the person within, trust the inner self.
Life in itself is a pool of feelings, sentiments, instincts, intuitions
inclinations.

Let the bonding and love be the essence of life. Trust will emanate.

My Soul.... .My Life.... .

Trust

Desire

I want you in abstract, I want you in concrete;
I want you in obvious, I want you in discrete.
I want you not in parts, I want you in complete;
Hold me in you, let not our love ever deplete.

She tells me to learn living without her,
I can't respond to our daughter's voice that I hear.
I wish I could tell you my life not to go,
But I know you won't accept my prayers so be it so.

I walked alone; I fell alone.
She was not there to clasp me,
She was not there in my woe.
I was astray even in light.

Let distance not create a chasm,
Let silence not create an impediment.
Let vexation never trounce our love.

Let our divinity not be afraid of risks,
Let selfies not replace our clicks.
Let your fragrance be in my persona gratus,
Let there be continuity in our status.

Let our souls not depart, let our hearts not shatter.
Let the hope to emerge never ever vanquish.

Let the cloud not loose its silver lining in this darkness,
Let our dots forever connect.
Let our silence always discourse,
Let our amalgamated souls never split.

I can never learn to walk without you,
I can never have a start that doesn't end with you;
I can never wipe my own salt,
Let there be no standstill, let the be no halt.

Hold me before I fall apart,
Hold us before I breathe my last.
Hold me before my tears dry,
Hold us before I speak my last.

My Soul.... .My Life.... .

As the sun rose,
I smiled as if it was a first sight,
As if the life was born today.
As if the eyes could see the dawn.
As if the first blossom of a flower,
As if the first breath of the heart.
As if the first chirp,
As if the first cry,
As if the first touch,
As if the first love.

There was light in the darkness,
There was fire in the sky.
There was calmness in the storm,
There was a fading twilight of states.
There was a stir in the sleep,
There was reflection in shadows.
I smiled as if it was a first sight,
As if the quietus cry,
As if the pounding laugh.
As if life, as if love.

My Soul.... .My Life.... .

Light

Words

The warmth we share are our words,
The love we carry are our words,
The silence of thoughts are words,
The agreement in our disagreement are our words.

The reverent silence in my eyes,
speaks through a thousand smile on your lips.

Let not the charm of its oracular divinity fritter away
with thoughts and expectations.

Let not our relation sour
in the race to win it over the world.

Let not the fragrance of our souls
dissipate in the fire of desire.

Let not our words speak adversely to our thoughts.

Let not our love disparage in the battle to win over our wrangle.

Let there be divinity till eternity,
let there be distance yet reach the horizon.

Let there be chaos yet serene.
Let there be silence yet words.
Let there be you and me
yet let there be WE.

My Soul.... .My Life.... .

Aperion.

An abstract, a mathematical number.
A symbol; limitless an illusion in reality.

A philosophy;
The Zeno of Elea and The Eudoxus of Cnidus,
A paradox; an enigma of thoughts
An argument, A thesis.
Anant, without destruction.

A thousand words, a simple thought;
A million of emotion, inexpressible.
I as I write for you, who it enwraps, as We transpires.

Desolate;
Love had no implication,
Life dawdled,
Thoughts had no eloquence,
Smile had no course.
Infinitely;
As we amassed,
Love found Life,
Silence could expatiate,
Souls were embellished with the beauty bejewelled.

My Love such is the spark of togetherness,
My Life such is the verve of the penchant,
Let there be divinity in thoughts,
Let there be purity in essence.
Let there be a fracas of love,
Let there be a tranquil in actions.

Let our dots be quaint,
Let there be togetherness,
Let there be finitism in the infinite.
Let there be We, let there be We.
Finitely Infinite
For Infinity, Aperion.

My Soul.... .My Life.... .

Infinity

Moments

A moment to cherish.
A thought to remember.
A smile that came, when my heart paused.
A light that blinked in my eye.
A thrill that ran within.
The breath stopped, words were lost,
thoughts were flowing, deep down the memory lane.
A day to remember, for us a day to revere, a day to behold.
Moments made memories; love made life.
Life made us souls.
Years might pass, life may depart.
Deep within somewhere it's there always there.

My Soul.... .My Life.... .

As I gather myself today,
My fingers tremble with thoughts known,
My heart shivers with consequences unknown.

My Lord, you made me,
You crafted my heart,
You designed my life,
You dressed my desires,
You painted my thoughts,
You winged me for actions.
If ever I faltered, if ever I failed,
You gathered my support,
You couraged my strength,
You battled my loss,
You won me Life.

As I stand today,
On the path unknown,
My faith courage's me to fight,
My loss strives me to win,
My belief makes me stand tall,
My support makes us behold,
My life never will fail.
My trust will always prevail.

So, as I rise today,
Smile when you see the sun,
Wink when the moon shines,
Laugh when the stars materialize.
They are your story; they are your battle.
Do not frail, do not falter.
Do not stop, do not pass.
Trust will prevail, Faith will attain.
You are crafted to fight,
You trialled to bounce.

As I gather myself today,
Certainly uncertain.

My Soul.... .My Life.... .

Courage

Together Forever

When the journey started,
You crossed path.
When love blossomed,
You gave fragrance to my heart.
When the world started to test,
You stood by.

When life was sailing,
You were there to row my boat.
When the sun shined bright,
You smiled together.
When times got difficult,
You taught to hold on.
When I was falling in the deep silence,
You held my hand.
When life gave us enough reasons to part,
You did hold on.
When it got darker,
You did spark the ray of light.
When I felt the end of road,
You showed me the horizon.

You are like a star who shines all night,
A sun that brightens my life.
Even if the sails get rough,
Even if our times get tough,
I know that there may be thousand reasons to fall,
You have that one reason to move all,
You have one promise to keep strong,
You have one love to love along.

My Soul.... .My Life.... .

Words which am always short of,
Expressions which my eyes are full of.
Love that my heart carries,
Wishes and desires that are always buried.

I wish we be the strength of ourselves.
Our silence be heard by our souls,
Our touch be felt by our heart,
Our love be felt within.

Let it be enduring,
Let not the silence diminish the spark of it,
Let distance not create a chasm,
Let our love be so esteem that the world extols it with envy.

Let me be your pride,
let me be your life.
Let me be ingrained,
just let me be there.

My Soul.... .My Life.... .

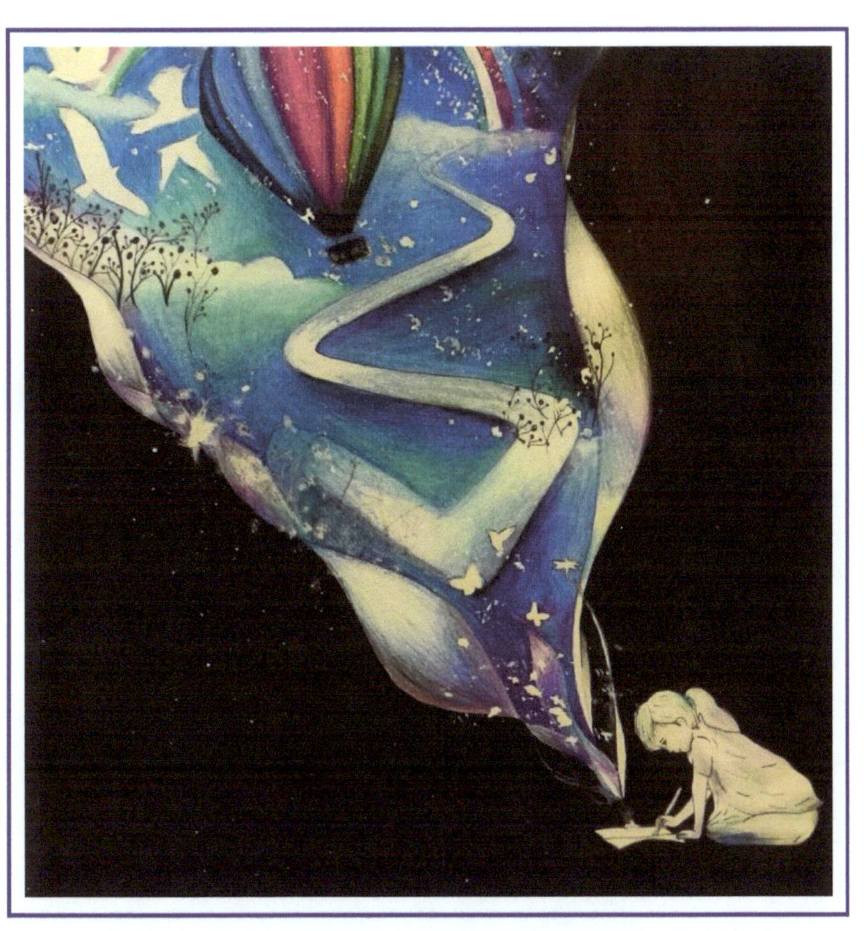

Thoughts

Pain

Pain is a significant factor of the most precious things of our life.

Where there's pain there's love.

Pain teaches us to believe in ourselves,
that each time you fall you can thrive back to stand.

Pain makes us believe in the goodness of life around us.

If everything was just impeccable,
then how would one perceive the strength within.
The constant effort to counterattack to achieve
what one's heart and soul desires.

Lost and Found.
Hate and Love.
Fall and Rise.
Loose and Achieve.
Tears and Happiness.
Pain and Love.
That is Life.

My Soul.... .My Life.... .

There is I who feels your pain,
There is you who flames that hurt,
There is I who believes in goodness,
There is you who believes in revenge.

There is I who believed in oneness,
There is you who broke the faith.
There is I who kept the flame going,
There is you who deluded my thoughts.

There is calmness in the storm,
There is dismay in the wave,
There is beguilement in the flow.

There is vexation in my sadness,
There is exasperation in my silence.
There is credence in my thoughts,
There is faith in the Divine.

There is a circle you will pass,
There is time you will perceive,
There is phase you will endure.

Behold,
As the solitude saddens you,
As the silence perturbs you.

There will be calmness in the storm,
There will be I who will have memories.
There will be you who will have remorse,
There will be calmness in the storm.

My Soul.... .My Life.... .

Calmness

Distance

It's the language of love.
Bridge it with our thoughts and the large expanse of space and time
is filled with moments, memories, passion, compassion, happiness.

Dreams are a portrayal of thoughts, feeling, emotions one carries through.
It bridges the distance between reality and mirage.

Let distance not create vexation, malaise, fretfulness in your inner self.

Let our soul speak our heart,
let our heart feel our soul,
let not distance be the reason for detachment of souls.

Distance is the test wherein two souls fall apart to be united within,
to be two poles away to bridge it with happiness, with love, with compassion.
That even the world says and speaks the language of our souls.

God tests us with his own ways, but when it's me and myself,
we touch his souls by our deeds, by our ways, by our love.
Cause it's we and we are together to bridge not to fall apart.
To create not to eradicate, to fill not to empty.
Life around us exists with mixed emotions,
let us fill it with the warmth of our hearts.

Let there be distance.
Yet there will be memories.
Yet there will be happiness.
Yet there will be love.

My Soul.... .My Life.... .

It was you, it was I
You were fire, I was burnt.
You were anger, I was offensed,
You were hated, I was torn.

You battled with others; I was distressed,
You were broken, I was hurt.
You were raged, I was disturbed,
You wanted justice, I was abandoned.

There was wrath, there was swedge,
There was loss, there was detachment,
There was disquiet, there was suffering,
There was departure, there was culmination.

I wanted life, you got me death,
I wanted happiness, you got me sorrow,
I wanted freedom, you got me bonding,
I wanted love, you got me hate.

Now,
There is no you, there is no I,
Still there is fire, still there is anger, still there is hate.
Now,
There will be no we. there will be no us.
There will be no you. There will be no I

Seperation

Alone

As I walk
My pain is unfelt,
My sorrows are blind,
My heart doesn't speak,
My eyes don't unfold,
My life doesn't fall,
My soul doesn't live,
My breath doesn't hold.
My scream doesn't plead.
My pain is unfelt, alone.

As I still walk

There is hope,
There is love,
There is silence,
There is Life,
There is Love.

My Soul.... .My Life.... .

As a day passes, I am alone,
As a night dwells, I am alone,
Life rows its boat as sails don't wait,
Darkness still prevails.
Waiting for the sun to rise,
To see its morning blaze.

An endless wait, an unfading silence
A falter in actions, a hiatus in speech.

Words gathered, muffled within,
Emotions unexpressed, dissimilarities questioned.

Imperfections celebrated.

Feelings unfelt, conscience questioned.

My Soul.... .My Life.... .

Chasm

Chaos

Just when there is one incident and God willing it hasn't affected you in anyways,
it hasn't harmed you in any means.

Realize.
There is a child who has lost a mother,
there is a mother who has lost her life,
there is a man who lost his love,
there is a Life who lost many Relations.

There is a sudden vacuum in today's morning, there is a killing silence in the night.

Many friends are besides today,
many in the family are by their side,
but tomorrow they will be gone.
Life will be empty, souls wandering, memories haunting.

My friend let us stand to be united, let us not dig mistakes,
let us not flaunt flaws, let us not sympathise Life's.

It maybe you tomorrow, it may be someone else by your side to console.
It may be some family suffering, it may be a relation alone, it may be a Life Little.

As I write this today, I feel so small in this world;
When we feel the nothingness of what we possess,
The dissatisfaction of faith,
The anger of insufficiency in possession,
The disillusion of Life.

Let us be fearing, let us be loving,
Let us not fight, let go of egos,
Let vexation not let revenge,
Let Faith not Faulter,
Let Life not Fail.
Let us be We.

My Soul.... .My Life.... .

When there is chaos everywhere,
When there is pathos in the air;
When we see things falling apart,
When we see eyes with a heavy heart.

Where a child is not spared,
Where a life is not cared.
Where a womb shies away.
Where anger has no control,
Where fights are the only chore.

When dignity is questioned,
Where a lady is dishonoured.
Where friendship is dubious,
Where relations work on rationales .

Where has the faith diminished?
Why has the trust fainted?
Where will the path reach?
Why can't we practice what we preach?

Trust the door ahead of you,
Hold the hands that follow you.
Walk the path, which is blind,
Maybe kindness is on the mind.

World where it is We,
Where I and You can together be;
Alone you have walked enough,
Let's blow the dust together.

Remember that it is He,
Mankind else would have never been.
Prayers are wishes He hears,
You ask and He is yours.
He created me, He created you.

A hand so warm,
A touch so tender;
A passion so strong,
A blessing so divine.
She's the woman,
She's the life;
Don't let her perish, don't let her frail.

When;
We stand together,
We change together;
We create together,
We will live together;
We are Life together.

Souls apart, Life shall depart.
Silence desolated.
Love perished.

My Soul.... .My Life.... .

World

Change

Life as it takes a walk in this world,
A chapter each day to unfold,
Change that was unexpected,
Change that was inevitable.

A morning had no light,
A truth that dawned upon.
A night without its shimmer,
A silk without its own cocoon.

Change as is inevitable.
My heart still awaits to unwind the truth,
My soul still mesmerises with dreams we shared.
The fragrance of memories touches me within,
My love you left me incomplete,
My life you left me indeed.

You failed to believe the goodness in me,
You failed to hold the consonance in me.
I asked you to walk the path, you left me astray,
I asked you to hold on to your heart, you broke me away,
I asked you to calm your soul, you silenced what I prayed.
I asked you to change for the goodness within,
You shyed away from being distinct.

My days are lonely,
My nights are dark,
My heart is shattered,
My soul is lost.

I wanted you to hold on,
I wanted to see the faith,
I wanted to see the rain,
I wanted to see the rain.

Today as I stand alone,
I still see the empty path,
I still see the entangled hearts,
I still see the smiling tears,
I still see the reflection clear.

Your mornings have changed,
Your prayers have silenced,
Your life remains unchanged,

I don't see the heart rise as I write today,
I don't see the dots shine as I speak today,
I don't see the silence smile as I sigh today.

Change, which is inevitable,
Couldn't change the love I breathe,
Couldn't take the soul I keep,
But could tear me deep beneath.

Days as have passed,
My smile has silenced,
My soul is now gone,
My heart doesn't know to breath alone.

As I breathe my last, I pray,
I see you each day,
I love you each day,
I feel you each day.

In the ray of my hope, I found you.
In the sermon of the Pope, I found you.

In the touch of dove, I found you.
In the clutch of love, I found you.

I found you when I reached my goal,
I found you when I searched my soul.

I found you at the end of time,
I found you in every rhythm and rhyme.

I found your clue in my daughter's smile,
I found your dew in my deserted isle.

In your reflection I found the womb that bore me,
In your intention I found everything just and only for me.

In your aura I found the pinnacle of grace,
In your heart I found my life's solace.

I found your flow in sacred waters,
I found your glow in the rising sun.

I found your beat in my heart within,
I found your heat in my breath and veins.

My Soul.... .My Life.... .

Existence

Life

So empty as I start, life has lessons to share.
Love, which was pure, love which was pious.
Life, which was complete, life which was happy.
The light of divinity was blazing like the morning sun,
The tranquil of love was shimmering like the evening moon.
Differences never could create distance,
Separation was far from even the existence of it.

Heart which beats within could feel the soul that showered its love upon.
Blessings flew miles apart as wind embraces up my arms.

A chasm so deep, A silence so strong.

Purity of love is buried within,
Incomplete is life as it breathes its bareness.
As the mornings glaze upon Life,
As the dusk falls on the shadow,
Distance has created disagreement.
Chasm so deep within,
Existence which is pyrrhic.

Heart still beats within, but souls dissipate to fondle,
Blessings are astray.

A chasm so deep, A silence so strong.

Love is not felt, Life has a saga to tell.
Walk as you stand, you have miles to pass,
Live as you breathe, you have nights to trounce,
Love as you encompass, benevolent as you be.

Life as it stands on the shore will watch you go by,
Proud will she be, far though she will be.
Maybe the distance, May be the absence,
May be the end, May be the beginning.
Life will have a saga to tell.

My Soul.... .My Life..... .

As I say I began to reminisce moments we shared,
We met to begin, to walk the path, to share this life.
The more we cruised the more we explored the depth of our hearts,
The more we shared, the more we learnt the purity of love.

A journey that made life
A journey that made souls
A journey that made us entangled in ourselves.

Life was filled with colours of happiness,
Life was happy in the ocean of relations.
The journey of a mother, a wife, a lover, a friend as I travelled,
Unprecedented were the moments we lived.

The journey has come to a standstill,
The path travelled has lost its course,
Life we lived is buried within.
Silence has taken a stupor.
Death awaits the fall.

Why did a mother fail,
Why was a wife misinterpreted,
Why was a lover questioned,
Why was a friend unexplainable.

The mourning's are over,
End has surpassed its emotions,
Life has moved its day,
Night has a saga to tell.

But,
The mother still stands on the endless path for his child to hold,
The wife still remembers the endless promises which were once told,
The lover still discovers the freshness of its soul,
A friend still awaits a friend to be told.

Life still awaits a new journey to unfold.

Journey

To a Mother

Who is a teacher, is a guide.
One who goes through all the ups and downs at every stage of life,
still standing tall to face the blow.

A young girl full of expectations, full of life, full of dreams,
a learner but still is a teacher.
A woman with family to nurture generations,
to teach the child to grow.

A generation moves
and she is still there waiting for her role to change.
She has her share in our lives in different ways.

She made a child walk, she made a child grow,
she taught him to face the world, She's still there.

Go embrace her, clasp her,
make her feel that life is incomplete without her,
no matter how complete you are.

That's a mother, a teacher,
a lesson you always want to learn all your life no matter how old you grow,
no matter the entire world is with you.

Mother is a sign of Strength, a sign of Love, a sign of Life.

My Soul.... .My Life.... .

I was not perfect, you were neither.
We can never be in life till we live.
We came together, we laughed together.
We loved together.

If ever my madness made you smile once,
If ever my thoughts made you think twice.
If ever you believed the goodness in me,
If ever it was for We.

Hold on,
Give up on everything which is unreal.
Hold on,
To the thoughts I trust.
Hold on,
Do not mistrust.
Hold on,
Before my heart breaks.
Hold on,
Before the poetry fails.

Don't hurt, don't analyse.
Close your eyes and shine and rise.
Smile when my madness embarrasses,
Love hard when there is love to be.
Live life the way it should be,
Don't let anger let go life.
Don't let love shatter in pain,
Don't let your life suffer even in vain.

Don't let my pride fail,
Don't let my life fail.
Please don't let my life fail.

As I say change is inevitable,
Change for the goodness in We.
Change for the love we call Life,
Change for it was me.

My Soul.... .My Life.... .

Hold On

Together Alone

Life as I write has come to a standstill,
Love as I feel has conceded to relinquish.

Day as it dawns don't see the mornings,
Maybe it is another reorientation of life.

Dusk as it sets in the darkness has sheath on my eyes,
For the blessings of the day have perished within.

Hearts which were entangled have shied away from beating,
Souls which were one have dissent from their existence.

A lover was questioned,
A mother was misconceived.
She paused in perplexity,
She was assumed to be ambivalent;
Her intent was questioned,
Her execution was rationalized.

She broke each time she elucidated,
Deep within a chasm of sorrow;
Lost was her existence,
Lost was her fervour.

A night has come,
She stands by the stars waiting to twinkle.
Unheard, unreal, transient,
Day she lived, night to travel;
Endless journey.

As she says Together Alone,
Walk as you stand;
Breathe as she desired,
Live as she wished;
Love as she expressed .
Change for the better in you, change for the we in you,
A mother is always there even when gone;
Blink and blessings reach Together Alone.

My Soul.... .My Life.... .

I have no words to say what I wish,
I have no actions which will make you believe that we exist,
I kept wandering on the land of nowhere,
I was neither here nor there,
Heart kept aching,
Mind kept reasoning.

My silence never spoke,
My love could never behold,
My fragrance was never felt,
My presence was always misinterpreted.

As I lay astray in the dark,
As I write on the blank path,
As I say what my silence says,

Let not the vexation within tear us apart,
Let not the sweetness of it turn sour,
Let not the fragrance be soul less,
Let not the heart be desolate,
Let not a mother fail,
Let not a child be lost,
Let not the cord detach.

Let the womb smile in pride,
Let the mirage be the mirror,
Let us be together,
Let us be we.
Let us be we.

My Soul.... .My Life.... .

Feelings

Maybe

A Day has passed, A Night has come.

Maybe you learned to row your boat alone,
Maybe you learnt to walk the path,
Maybe you learned to defy your soul,
Maybe you stood tall without support.

But,

Maybe the shadow has a silver lining throwing its light in water,
Maybe it's the footprints which are guiding you on your path,
Maybe it's the love which matured to renounce its rights,
Maybe it's the windfall of strength you left behind.

May be a child has grown, May be a mother has accomplished.

Maybe love has ceased.
Maybe heart has departed,
Maybe life has moved.

Let it be going, let it be gone, let it just pass, let it just stay.

My Soul.... .My Life.... .

Like a dry well waiting for rain.
Like a big swell blown over the shore.
Like a single star in the mighty sky.
Like a fire spark in the disquiet cold.
Like a drop of tear from the heart.
Like a lonely soul in the throng.

My Soul.... .My Life.... .

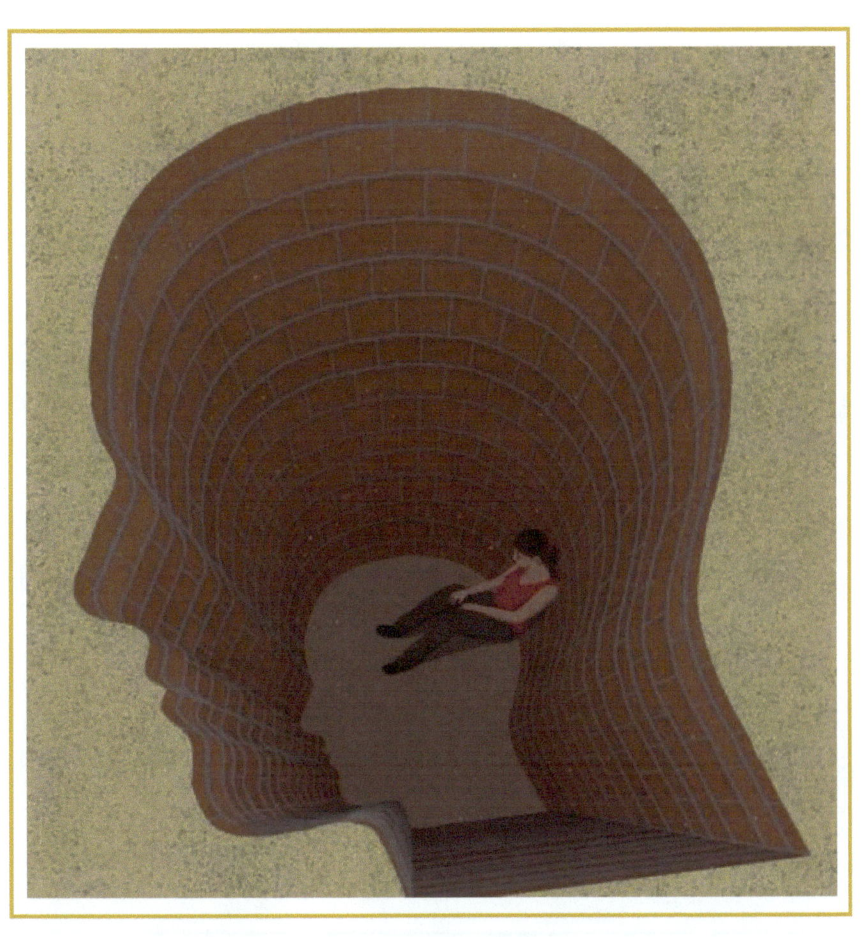

Emptiness

Loosing

A mother who never carried you in her body
but touched your soul beyond this world.
A mother whose life wasn't complete without the soul.
A mother who lived for you maybe not complete.
A mother who lost her own self in the battle to win her son.
A mother who wished to see her son much higher than her imaginations.
A mother who nurtured her love for you maybe beyond her potential,
A mother who failed never to rise again,
A mother who is shattered beyond belief,
A mother who breathed her last
when her son was not there to carry her in his heart.

My Soul.... .My Life.... .

The dawn was dark,
Sun as it shined bright failed to shower on its light.
Maybe the darkness of the night quelled itself on.

Maybe blessing which gushed didn't reach its destination,
Maybe life as it began failed to endeavour its goal.
Hearts pushed its thread to death,
Souls which were one chose to wander in the dark.

Silence went unheard,
Words were misconstrued.
Elucidations were disputed,
Tears were judgemental .

Hatred prevailed; Love was astray.

Shattered are the dreams,
Unhinged are thoughts,
Wishes are barren.

As emptiness flew from within,
As eyes were incomplete,
As Life was desolate,
Soul whispered,
It's the Beginning of an End.

Behold as the beginning wished to
Embark on the journey unseen,
Live as you rise, Love as I wished.
Begin so that it never ends.

My Soul.... .My Life.... .

Beginning to End

Goodbyes

As the sunsets today, dreams rise in my eyes.
As the moon is bright, my wishes are whispered.
The dusk is falling on the shadow of my heart.
The sparkle of night unfolds the thoughts of my soul.
Wishes fulfilled and unfilled, life complete though empty.

Shadows holding hands, hearts entwine our souls.
The world is calling to bid goodbye to the days gone,
for a new day to arrive.

The twilight today has a saga to tell,
The dusk falls on moments that made memories.

As the world is eager to await the dawn of the new era,
Prayers pour from my eyes to fulfil what we wished for.
Not to wish goodbye to the past year,
But to bow down before the almighty
to thank the precious moments we lived,
For happiness He gave, for the love He showered.

As the dawn awakens a million lives,
My wishes reach you though distant and far,
I pray for the good in you,
I pray for the best for you.
May the New beginning bring more calmness, more tranquil,
more placate in your actions.

Goodbyes are painful but reminiscent.
May goodbyes be moments to cherish and moments to revere.
May life be a celebration for moments to come.

Wishes to wish a new era to unfold.

My Soul.... .My Life.... .

As the sun rose today,
I knew the dark night was coming,
As the birds chirped,
I wished they never silenced.
As the empty paths filled,
I could hear chaos coming,
As the cold wind passed,
I could feel the hurt of the heat.

Your absence showed failure,
Your silence showed betrayal.
It was a heart that was breaking,
It was a dream that was dying.

Dusk slowly fell upon,
As I still awaited, for a star to shine.
A hope that was still alive,
A tear that would bring a smile.

An end that would bring a new beginning,
A night that would bring a new dawn.
A spring that would bring a new day.
A death that would bring a new life.

My Soul.... .My Life.... .

End

www.ingramcontent.com/pod-product-compliance
Lightning Source LLC
LaVergne TN
LVHW021335160826
845679LV00008B/1358

9798896322412